BE BOLD! BE BRAVE!

¡SÉ AUDAZ, SÉ VALIENTE!

11 Latinas who made U.S. History
11 Latinas que hicieron historia en Estados Unidos

Written by: Naibe Reynoso

Illustrated by: Jone Leal

Publisher's Cataloging-in-Publication Data
Names: Reynoso, Naibe, author. | Leal, Jone, illustrator.
Title: Be bold! Be brave! Sé audaz! Sé valiente! : 11 Latinas who made U.S. history , 11 Latinas que hicieron historia en los Estados Unidos / Naibe Reynoso ; illustrated by Jone Leal.
Description: Includes bibliographical references. | Los Angeles, CA: Con Todo Press, 2019.
Summary: A bilingual book that highlights 11 Latinas who excelled in their professional fields and made U.S. history in medicine, science, sports, art and politics.
Identifiers: ISBN 978-1-7337103-0-5
Subjects: LCSH Hispanic American women--Biography--Juvenile literature. | Women--Biography--Juvenile literature. | CYAC Hispanic American women--Biography. | Women--Biography. | BISAC JUVENILE NONFICTION / Biography & Autobiography / Cultural, Ethnic & Regional | JUVENILE NONFICTION / Biography & Autobiography / Women
Classification: LCC E184.S75 .R495 2019 DDC 973/.04/68092--dc23
Library of Congress Control Number: 2019901583

Printed in the United States of America

First Printing, 2019

ISBN-13: 978-1-7337103-0-5

Translated by Maria Garcia and Vanessa Saenz
Graphic Designer Tania Peregrino

www.contodopress.com

CON TODO
PRESS

DEDICATION

*For my Mother, Hortencia Reynoso Rodriguez and my daughter
Giselle Jacqueline Carrillo, who have taught me and
encouraged me to Be Bold, and Be Brave....*

AUTHORS NOTE:

As a journalist with over twenty years of professional experience in television, radio, online and other media platforms, it has always been important for me to tell stories of my community. When I looked for books to read to my children, I noticed a lack of children's publications highlighting Latina women who have greatly contributed to U.S. history. I hope this book inspires young little girls of all races and ages to pursue their passions, and provides role models for whatever career they dream of. And I hope it sparks conversations between young children and their parents about their future professional endeavors.

NOTA DE LA AUTORA:

Como periodista con más de veinte años de experiencia profesional en televisión, radio, online y otras plataformas, siempre ha sido importante para mí contar historias de mi comunidad. Cuando busqué libros para leerles a mis hijos, noté la falta de publicaciones infantiles que destacáran a las mujeres latinas que han contribuido enormemente a la historia de los EE. UU. Espero que este libro inspire a las niñas de todas las razas y edades a perseguir sus pasiones, y proporcione modelos a seguir para cualquier carrera que sueñen. Espero también que despierte conversaciones entre padres e hijos sobre sus futuros esfuerzos profesionales.

THIS BOOK BELONGS TO:

_____

Los padres de Rita Moreno- ¡Una costurera y un granjero!
Pero ella siempre amó la actuación, y quiso dedicarse a ello.

¡Canta! ¡Baila! Es versátil en varias cosas.
¡Es una mujer en verdad talentosa!

Un Tony, un Emmy, un Grammy y un Oscar están entre
  sus premios,
Pero el mejor de todos, es haber alcanzado sus sueños.

RITA MORENO
Oscar-Winning Actress

Rita Moreno's mom was a seamstress and her dad a farmer,
but she always knew she wanted to be a performer!

She's very talented, as a matter of fact,
and can do many things like sing, dance and act!

She has won an Emmy, a Grammy, and a Tony Award!
She's even won an Oscar. She's truly adored!

A Lisa Fernández le gustan los deportes de todo tipo.
De niña jugaba softbol en un pequeño equipo.

A los 8 años inició su pasión por ser una gran atleta.
Y con mucha dedicación … ¡logró su meta!

Practicó muchos años para alcanzar su sueño:
¡Una medalla olímpica llevar en su cuello!

LISA FERNÁNDEZ
Olympic Gold Medalist

Lisa Fernandez enjoys many sports.
She likes basketball, softball, and games of all sorts.

Athletics is a passion she's had since age eight.
She never gave up and soon became great!

She practiced for years to accomplish her dream,
winning gold medals with the Olympic Softball team!

Selena nació en una pequeña ciudad de Tejas.
¡Con su carisma y tenacidad abrió muchas puertas!

Cantó en inglés y en español, traspasando fronteras.
El ser bilingüe en el escenario, fue de las primeras.

Cantante, empresaria y hasta diseñadora,
pero más que nada, ¡una mujer luchadora!

SELENA
Latina Icon

Selena was born in a small city in Texas.
She grew to be famous because her voice was infectious!

She balanced two cultures which is no easy feat,
And sang in English and Spanish while dancing to the beat!

From fashion, to music to movies and more,
she became a role model like no one before.

Ellen Ochoa fue la primera latina al espacio llegar.
¡En el transbordador Discovery viajó a tan lejano lugar!

Sobresaliente en temas de matemáticas, física y ciencia,
Se graduó como ingeniera, ¡es una eminencia!

¡También es piloto, flautista e inventora!
Una mujer como tú, soñadora…

ELLEN OCHOA
Astronaut and Inventor

Ellen Ochoa was the first Latina to go into space!
She traveled on the shuttle Discovery to that faraway place!

In college, she studied to become an engineer,
learning about physics, science and the atmosphere!

She's an inventor, a flutist, and even a pilot!
And you can be too if you really desire it!

¡Bibliotecaria, autora y titiritera!
A Pura le encantaba contar cuentos a pequeños dondequiera.

Su pasión fue leer y promover la lectura,
algo necesario si quieres algún día ser una gran figura.

Pura escribió muchos libros sobre folklore y tradición.
¡Contar historias en inglés y español fue su principal misión!

PURA BELPRÉ
Librarian/Author

Librarian, author and talented puppeteer,
Pura loved telling stories to children far and near!

Her passion was to inspire children to read,
which is important and necessary if you ever want to lead.

Pura wrote many books about folklore and tradition.
Telling stories in English and Spanish was her
     principal mission!

A Sonia Sotomayor desde niña le gustaba estudiar.
Dedicada a su educación para un mejor futuro forjar.

Fue a la Universidad de Princeton y se convirtió en abogada,
cumpliendo sus metas por ser una alumna aplicada.

Ahora es juez en la Corte Suprema, ¡un trabajo muy importante!
Toma decisiones sobre la ley federal, ¡es una mujer brillante!

SONIA SOTOMAYOR
U.S. Supreme Court Justice

Sonia Sotomayor was very good at school.
She studied hard, and got good grades, and followed all the rules.

She later went to Princeton and became a lawyer then a judge.
Always having bigger dreams—on that she would not budge.

Now she makes decisions ruling on Federal law.
She's a Supreme Court justice, the biggest job of all!

PRINCETON

¿Te gusta contar historias? ¿Has pensado en ser cronista?
Como María Hinojosa, una gran periodista.

Puedes ser reportera en radio o televisión,
escribiendo sobre tu comunidad, si esa es tu pasión.

Los periodistas como María narran historias de justicia y unidad.
¡Relatos que inspiran, nos informan y nos dan más claridad!

MARIA HINOJOSA
Award-Winning Journalist

Do you like to tell stories or perhaps write your own?
How about saying them out loud on a microphone?

Journalists write and tell stories about their community.
Many of them spotlight bravery, justice and unity!

Like Maria Hinojosa who chose that career,
telling stories that inspire, inform us and make things more clear.

¿Qué te gustaría ser de grande? ¿Ingeniera, científica o profesora?
¿O posiblemente convertirte en una gran doctora?

Como Antonia Novello, una pediatra cariñosa,
que trató a niños como ella, que nacieron con una condición dolorosa.

Fue Cirujana General de los Estados Unidos durante su profesión.
Nombrada por el presidente ¡Doctora de la Nación!

ANTONIA NOVELLO
First Female U.S. Surgeon General

Have you thought of a career as an engineer or author?
Or perhaps you'd study medicine to become a great doctor?

Like Antonia Novello who became a pediatrician,
to help kids like her, born with a painful condition.

She also served as Surgeon General—an important position.
Appointed by the President, it's our country's top physician!

Judy Baca es una pintora, una artista de gran carrera.
¡También es académica, muralista y pionera!

Cuenta la historia de varias comunidades a través de sus murales,
sin importar raza, o clases sociales.

Sus pinturas narran historias usando colores brillantes.
¡El arte es necesario para conversaciones importantes!

JUDY BACA
Artist/Muralist/Scholar

Judy Baca is a painter, an artist with a vast career!
She's also a scholar, a muralist and community pioneer!

She paints on city walls, depicting people of all races.
Using color and heart to tell stories in public spaces.

Her murals tell the history of social transformation.
Indeed art is needed for important conversations!

Hilda Solís fue la primera en su familia en graduarse de la universidad.
Hoy es una mujer exitosa que ayuda a su comunidad.

Fue Secretaria de Trabajo y en la Casa Blanca colaboró.
También estuvo en el Congreso y ¡como política se destacó!

Hilda crea leyes que nos ayudan a progresar.
Justa, trabajadora y honrada, ¡ayuda a muchos a triunfar!

HILDA SOLIS
Politician

Hilda Solis was the first in her family to graduate from college.
She's helped her community with all of her knowledge.

She's worked in the California Senate, the White House and
    Congress,
making laws that are fair and help the country
    progress!

The first Latina to serve in the U.S. Cabinet-
    she was Secretary of Labor.
She made sure the laws were in the
    workers' favor!

Dolores Huerta, fiel defensora de los derechos humanos,
luchó para que los campesinos tuvieran mejores salarios.

Dolores alza su voz, cuando es necesario.
Su activismo la ha llevado hablar en grandes escenarios.

Una madre que lucha con fuerza, convicción y talento,
¡Su compromiso con el pueblo está presente en todo momento!

DOLORES HUERTA
Activist

Dolores Huerta fought to try and make things fair,
using her voice with strength, conviction and flair!

She's talked to lots of people on many stages,
and made sure that farm workers received better wages!

She's an activist and mother who fights for equality,
making sure everyone's life is of the utmost quality!

YOU / TÚ

Although we've reached the end of this book,
YOUR story is next! Just go to the mirror and take a look!

If there are things in the world you want to see different,
you can change them for sure, just don't be indifferent!

Be brave, be bold, and be courageous,
because YOUR destiny is also greatness!

Like all of these women who weren't afraid!
So go out into the world and just remember, be BRAVE!

Ahora comienza tu propia historia: ve y mírate en el espejo.
¡Y verás que hay grandeza en tu propio reflejo!

Si hay cosas en el mundo que quieres ver diferente,
Puedes cambiarlas, ¡no seas indiferente!

Sólo recuerda: ¡Sé audaz! ¡Sé valiente!
Porque tu historia también es grande y es la siguiente.

¡TÚ eres valiosa! ¡Muéstrate segura y fuerte!
Como estas mujeres, al mundo hazle frente.

NAIBE REYNOSO
Author

Naibe Reynoso is a multi-Emmy award-winning journalist with over two decades of career experience. Her work has been seen in CNN Español, France 24, Reelz Channel, Univision, Telemundo/KWHY, and Fox News Latino to name a few. She is also a board member of the prestigious Peabody Awards. She graduated from UCLA with a degree in Sociology, and a double concentration in Psychology and Chicano Studies. This is her first children's book. It was written to help inspire the next generation of little girls, and highlight Latina trailblazers. She lives in her native, Los Angeles, California with her teenage daughter, young son and husband Jeff.

To learn more about the author, go to naibereynoso.com or follow her on Instagram @naibereynoso

JONE LEAL
Illustrator

Jone Leal, also known as "jonewho" is a Venezuelan illustrator who loves to work with children's book illustrations and women empowerment. She has over 5 years of experience in the area. When she's not drawing, you can find her sewing while listening to her favorite music. To see more of her work visit jonewho.com

To learn more about CON TODO PRESS
visit contodopress.com or follow @contodopress